Timeline of Key Events

1584-1590
Three separate voyages send English settlers to Roanoke, Virginia (now North Carolina).

May 13, 1607
The colonists choose Jamestown Island as the site for settlement.

April 10, 1606
James I grants a charter to the Virginia Company to establish colonies in Virginia.

March 24, 1603
Queen Elizabeth I of England dies; King James VI of Scotland also becomes James I of England.

May 1-4, 1607
Exploring parties sail up the James River in search of a good place to settle, following the instructions given to them by Virginia Company officials in London.

September 10, 1608

John Smith is elected president of the Virginia Council.

March 10, 1614

John Rolfe sends his first shipment of tobacco to England.

1620

The Pilgrims land at Plymouth to establish a colony in what is at this time called Northern Virginia.

September 1609

John Smith is injured in a gunpowder explosion. He sails back to England in October, never to return to the Chesapeake area of Virginia.

Fall 1607

More than half the colonists die: most from disease and starvation, a few from fighting with Native Americans.

Map of the First Settlements

Why did thousands of European men and women leave their work, homes, and families to settle in the "unknown" land of America in the early 17th century?

Some simply hoped to get rich quickly. There was a ready market in Europe for American goods, especially tobacco. Some ordinary working people hoped to make a better life away from the poverty and strict social barriers that oppressed them in Europe.

However, most of these pioneering settlers did not succeed in their aims. They did not have the knowledge or skills to survive in an unknown environment, where soils, plants, weather, and wildlife were so different from those back home. Their seeds would not grow, so many went hungry and had no resistance to diseases. Most died. Some were killed by Native Americans upset about the takeover of their land. However, a few tough individuals survived and built villages that flourished, as settlers learned how to live in this strange New World.

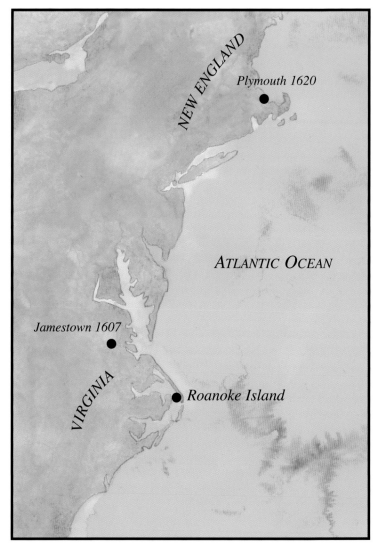

Author:

Jacqueline Morley studied English literature at Oxford University. She has taught English and history and now works as a freelance writer. She has written historical fiction and nonfiction for children.

Artist:

David Antram was born in Brighton, England, in 1958. He studied at Eastbourne College of Art and then worked in advertising for fifteen years before becoming a full-time artist. He has illustrated many children's nonfiction books.

Series Creator:

David Salariya was born in Dundee, Scotland. He has illustrated a wide range of books and has created and designed many new series for publishers both in the UK and overseas. In 1989, he established The Salariya Book Company. He lives in Brighton, England, with his wife, illustrator Shirley Willis, and their son, Jonathan.

Editor: **Michael Ford**

Assistant Editor: **Charlene Dobson**

© The Salariya Book Company Ltd MMXIII

No part of this publication may be reproduced in whole or in part, or stored in a retrieval system, or transmitted in any form or by any means, electronic, mechanical, photocopying, recording, or otherwise, without written permission of the publisher. For information regarding permission, write to the copyright holder.

Published in Great Britain in 2013 by
The Salariya Book Company Ltd
25 Marlborough Place, Brighton BN1 1UB

ISBN-13: 978-0-531-25946-7 (lib. bdg) 978-0-531-24502-6 (pbk.)

All rights reserved.
Published in 2013 in the United States
by Franklin Watts
An imprint of Scholastic Inc.
Published simultaneously in Canada.

A CIP catalog record for this book is available from the Library of Congress.

Printed and bound in Shanghai, China.
Printed on paper from sustainable sources.
Reprinted in MMXVIII.
13 14 15 R 22 21 20 19 18

SCHOLASTIC, FRANKLIN WATTS, and associated logos are trademarks and/or registered trademarks of Scholastic Inc., 557 Broadway, New York, NY 10012.

PAPER FROM
SUSTAINABLE
FORESTS

You Wouldn't Want to Be an American Colonist!

Written by
Jacqueline Morley

Illustrated by
David Antram

Created and designed by
David Salariya

A Settlement You'd Rather Not Start

Franklin Watts®
An Imprint of Scholastic Inc.
NEW YORK • TORONTO • LONDON • AUCKLAND • SYDNEY
MEXICO CITY • NEW DELHI • HONG KONG
DANBURY, CONNECTICUT

Contents

Introduction

It's the end of the 16th century and Elizabeth I is queen of England. She has defended England against Spain, the biggest power in Europe. Spain is strong and very rich. They have silver mines in America, the new land discovered by Christopher Columbus a century ago. The Spanish funded Columbus's voyages and claimed America as theirs.

However, America is huge and Spain can't control it all. The French, Dutch, and English are there too, exploring the north and staying out of Spain's way. They also want America's gold and silver. This sounds good to you. You want to join the next trip to start an English colony. If you knew what hardships and struggles lay ahead, you certainly wouldn't want to be an American colonist!

Colonist sea routes, 1607

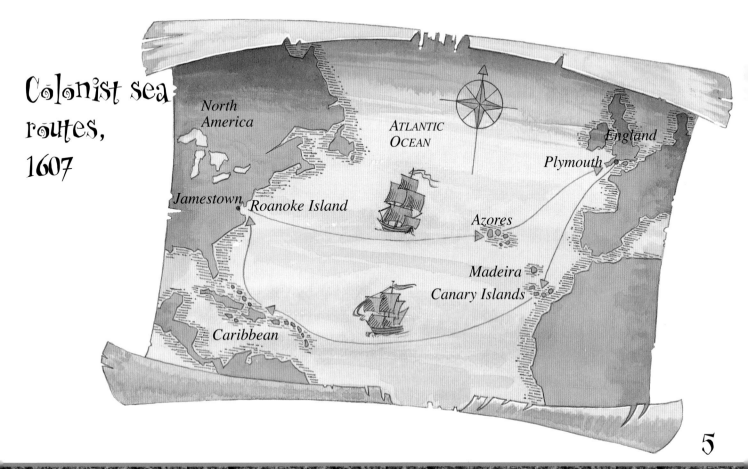

North America

ATLANTIC OCEAN

England

Plymouth

Jamestown

Roanoke Island

Azores

Madeira

Canary Islands

Caribbean

Virginia – A Bit of History

Walter Raleigh is Queen Elizabeth's favorite courtier. He tells her he has found the perfect site for the colony she hopes to set up in America. He sends out an exploratory mission. They return with reports of a warm, fertile spot on the North Atlantic shores of America. This spot is far from any Spanish settlement. The Queen is delighted. She dubs Raleigh a knight and declares that the new territory will be named Virginia (in her honor, since she is known as the "Virgin Queen"). Raleigh gathers an expedition of around 500 male settlers and sets sail in 1585. But their colony isn't a success. What goes wrong?

Rise, Sir Walter, and tell me of this paradise.

THE RIGHT SITE. Raleigh knows he has to find a site first. In 1583, his half-brother had set out with 260 men, but had no idea where to land. He drowned at sea.

Handy Hint

To persuade people to fund a trip, suggest that they will make a fortune from capturing Spanish cargo ships along the way.

PARADISE FOUND? The men Raleigh sent to find a site describe America as a paradise. Ripe grapes grow wild and the natives are friendly.

NATIVES. They bring two native people back to England to learn their language. Londoners stare at them in amazement.

SEVEN SHIPS. Raleigh raises a fleet of seven ships to take his colonists across the Atlantic Ocean. He does not go himself, but puts two tough, experienced commanders in charge.

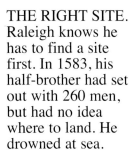

The Lost Colony

R aleigh's colonists settle on an island called Roanoke. They bully the native Algonquian tribe for food and to find out where gold can be found. The colonists take hostages and burn villages. When a supply ship doesn't arrive, the colonists sail home. In 1587, a second expedition, led by John White, includes women. The Algonquians are hostile, so White sails home for supplies. The colonists left behind are told to leave a message if they leave the settlement. When White returns three years later, he finds the buildings torn down and the settlement abandoned. The word "Croatoan" has been carved on a post, but nobody knows what has happened to the colonists.

RECKLESS ACTS. When friendly Algonquians steal a settler's cup, the hotheaded leaders of the first trip destroy the natives' village and burn all of their crops.

REVENGE. The Algonquians do not forgive. One of White's team is shot with 16 arrows while fishing for crabs.

FIRST BABY. White's daughter has a baby at Roanoke and names her Virginia. She is the first English colonist born in America.

Provisions you'll need:

The Voyage Out

It's 1606, and despite the Roanoke disaster some optimistic London merchants form the Virginia Company to finance a trading colony in Virginia. They are sending out three ships, the largest only 72 feet (22 m) long. You are one of 144 settlers crammed on board. With the stormy Atlantic Ocean threatening to sink the boat, you're already thinking this was a bad decision. If you're lucky, you will spend two months at sea. However, the trip can take up to six months if storms blow your ship off course.

SALTED MEAT and fish, dried fruit, beans, and hard biscuits are all you eat.

FRESH SUPPLIES. The ships take a southerly route via the Caribbean Islands. You can buy fresh fruit, vegetables, and meat there.

Mooooo

Cluck Cluck

Snort

10

At least you're not paying for this terrible journey. Those colonists who do pay will be given land in the new colony. You can't afford the fare, so you have promised to work for the company for seven years instead. There aren't any private rooms on board so you sleep on the floor of the smelly lower deck.

Third Time Is a Charm?

April 1607 — Virginia at last! The ships explore a river to find a good place to settle. The leaders argue all the time despite clear orders from the company. The site must be healthy, fertile, and easy to defend. It also needs to have a clear view of ships approaching from the sea, in case the Spanish attack. Luckily, the settlers find a place where ships can dock close to the bank. The land is low and unoccupied. It's almost like an island, so it's hard to attack from land. It's a perfect spot to start the colony.

That way…

No, this way, you fool!

Handy Hint

If you find a place that local people don't seem to want, ask yourself why. There may be drawbacks you don't notice.

GET RICH QUICK. Some colonists won't do heavy work. They are "gentlemen" and in England they didn't have to work. They've come to make a quick fortune from gold and won't obey orders.

Problems with the site:

SWAMP LAND. Most of the land is swamp. The rest consists of a thin layer of good soil over muddy clay.

CRAZY CLIMATE. The weather is unpredictable. Sometimes it's hot and humid, with sudden violent winds and thunderstorms.

MOSQUITOES breed in the swamps and carry deadly yellow fever. No one realizes this at the time.

Settling In

The new settlement is called Jamestown after England's new king, James I. Tents are put up and the work begins. Soon your hands blister and bleed from chopping trees. You're not used to all this hard work! The goal is to build a strong fort. The colony was almost wiped out in the first few days. Two hundred Algonquian warriors launched an ambush while everyone was working and unarmed. You would all be dead if cannons fired from the ships hadn't scared the attackers off.

UNDER ATTACK. A tent offers no protection. A man and a boy are killed and 10 colonists are wounded when the camp is attacked.

WATCH OUT when you leave the fort to relieve yourself in the bushes. There could be a nasty surprise waiting for you.

ARMOR IS USELESS. It's hot and very heavy to wear. Enemies will know exactly where you are because it is noisy.

I thought I was coming to paradise!

Oops!

Handy Hint

Take advice from friendly locals. One suggestion is to cut the long grass around the fort because enemies can hide there.

SPANISH INVASION. Hostile neighbors are not your only concern. Cannons are now mounted at each corner of the fort in case the Spanish attack.

DEATH TOLL. Many colonists become sick from yellow fever or by drinking polluted water from the river. By September, half of them are dead.

LEADERS FIGHT and accuse each other of planning rebellions within the colony. One of them is tried, found guilty, and shot.

The Algonquians – Friends or Foes?

There are many different tribes that live in villages nearby. They build houses out of bark or matting attached to a framework of poles. They grow sweet corn, which is their main food source, and hunt and fish. They do not know how to make metal or glass, so they are fascinated by the knives and colorful glass beads you bring to trade. Friendlier tribes are eager to exchange food for these shiny trinkets — at first.

Jar made from hollowed gourd

ALGONQUIANS' clothes are made of animal skins. The woman has her arm in a sling set with tiny shells. The shells are used as money.

WOMEN DO THE FARMING and weed the corn. One hides in a shelter to scare birds away.

ENGLISH WAYS of farming do not work here. Plows snag on tree roots and wheat won't sprout.

STARVING. Winter comes and you have no food. The Algonquians have none to spare.

A CAPTIVE shows you how to grow corn. Plant a few seeds in mounds of soil.

Exploring the Territory

The Virginia Company wants to make lots of money. It expects the colonists to discover where gold can be mined and to find the great lake that everyone believes is a shortcut to China! A team led by a fiery and tough-minded colonist, Captain John Smith, goes out to explore. He returns alone with a hair-raising story. Captured and condemned to death, he is saved in the nick of time by an Algonquian princess who begs her father to spare his life.

The adventures of John Smith:

1. EXPLORING a narrow river, the team's barge is blocked by overhanging branches. Smith then decides to continue by canoe.

2. AMBUSHED by hostile bowmen, Smith uses his guide (a friendly Algonquian) as a shield. He manages to escape, but is captured when he falls into a bog.

3. TAKEN PRISONER. The captured Smith is paraded around villages by dancing warriors, who lead him to the great chief Powhatan.

4. POWHATAN, the mighty chief of many tribes, believes colonists are a threat to his people. After questioning Smith, he condemns him to death by clubbing.

Handy Hint

Impress your captors with your "magic." Smith shows them his compass which "knows" where north is.

Put down your clubs.

Gulp!

SAVED! As the executioners raise their clubs, Powhatan's young daughter Pocahontas throws herself on Smith to protect him. Taking this as an omen, Powhatan spares his life and swears that Smith is his brother from now on.

19

Supply Ships – A Blessing or a Curse?

The Virginia Company sends out supply ships to the colony. Bad weather can delay them for months. Some never arrive at all. When they do, you might wish they hadn't. Their crews don't know how hard life can be over here. The captain of the first ship stays for 14 weeks looking for gold. He keeps his crew fed all this time on supplies meant for you. The crew spends its time trading with the Algonquians and, having much more to offer than the colonists, they drive the price of local food sky-high. You are glad to see the supply ships leave. Next comes a shipment of new settlers, mostly unskilled – just more useless extra mouths to feed when you're already starving!

TROUBLE. Some new arrivals look like troublemakers that England wants to get rid of. They come over expecting an easy life.

RATIONS. In England, the new settlers heard that everything is going well at Jamestown. The daily ration of boiled barley comes as a shock to them.

NO GOLD. No one finds any gold. Rocks sent home for testing are worthless. The captain has no luck panning the river for gold either.

TOOLS FOR FOOD. Many tools disappear from the fort's storage house. Desperate colonists steal them to buy food from the sailors.

IT'S HARD watching the lazy crew eating the food supplies. The captain refuses to unload any food unless he has enough for his long voyage home.

Handy Hint

Put a lock on the storage house to prevent tools and supplies from being stolen.

This lot don't look as though they'll be much help!

The Struggle to Survive

Captain Smith is in charge now. Unlike previous leaders, he makes even the laziest gentlemen work. They build, plant fields, and dig proper wells. The colony also has to satisfy the Virginia Company, which is demanding goods to sell in England to cover the cost of sending you supplies. Timber is the only raw material. You turn it into clapboard to send home on the next voyage.

Setbacks:

Sniff

JANUARY 1608. A terrible fire breaks out in the fort. Almost all the buildings are destroyed and need to be rebuilt.

BROWN RATS that escaped from the supply ships have bred in huge numbers. They eat half the corn reserves in the storage house.

SPRING 1609. Food is so scarce that Smith sends a third of the colonists down the river to see if they can live on oysters from the riverbed.

Aaargh!

Woof!

Squaark!

Handy
Hint

Keep a fishing
net handy.
You won't
catch many
fish with your
frying pan.

HARD TIMES. Explorations
go on, but life is hard when
you're huddled under a tarp.
You're cold, wet, and scared
that enemies are all around.

STRANGE CREATURES. You
never know what you'll meet in
a strange land. When Captain
Smith is stung by a stingray, it is
so painful he thinks he is dying.

FINAL DEMAND. In a
furious letter, Smith tells the
Virginia Company to send
him people with useful skills
and that the trees are not
suitable for clapboard.

23

Famine and Starvation

It's winter in 1609. A drought has made the crops fail. The Algonquians have little to eat and there's no food at Jamestown. The storehouse is empty and raiding the Algonquians for food has made them bitter enemies. You've eaten the horses, dogs, cats, and rats. You've even boiled your boots, belts, and every scrap of leather for food! People stagger into the woods in search of snakes or edible roots. Most will never return. You bury bodies daily and you even suspect that some colonists will dig them up again to eat!

YOU CAN DIE of famine in the safety of the fort or risk your life outside in search of food. Algonquian warriors are waiting to pick you off.

BROKEN PROMISES. Smith has returned to England and Powhatan is no longer friendly. He won't sell you corn and wants to drive the colonists from the land.

WARNINGS. Colonists who try to steal corn are found dead, their mouths stuffed with bread. It's a warning from the Algonquians.

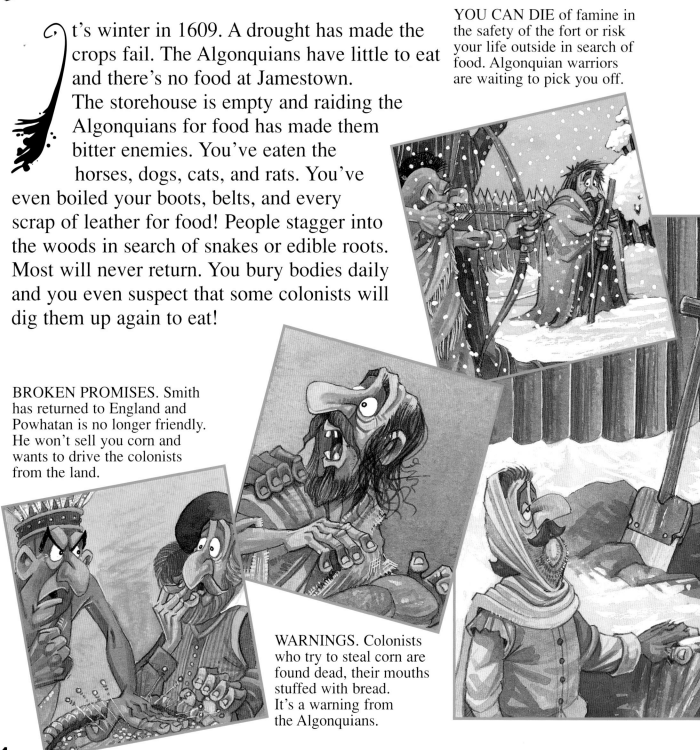

HUNGER drives some people crazy. A man is convicted for killing his wife. He chopped her up, salted the pieces, and ate most of her before he was caught. His sentence is to be burned alive.

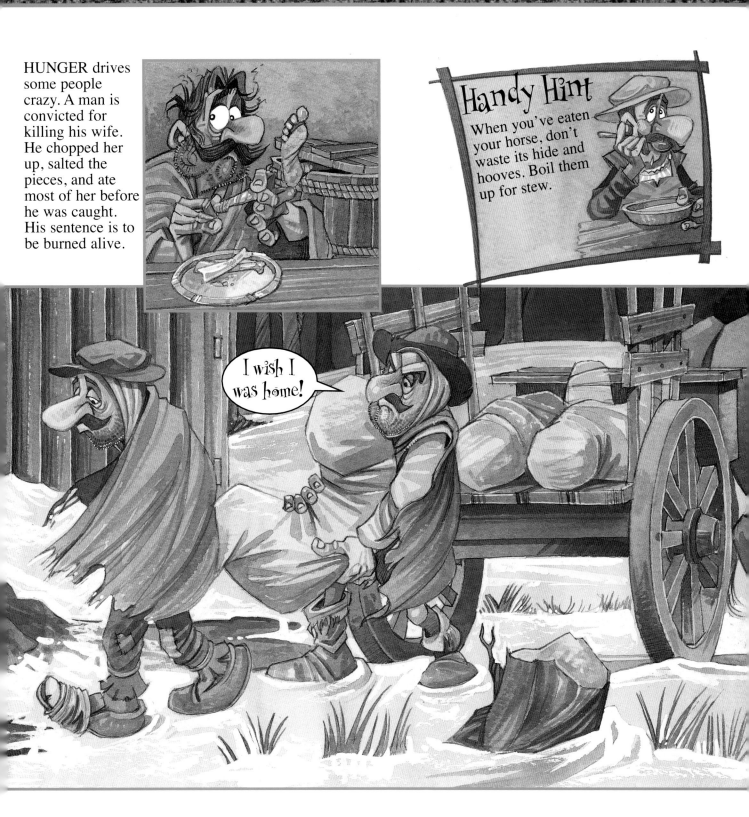

Handy Hint

When you've eaten your horse, don't waste its hide and hooves. Boil them up for stew.

I wish I was home!

The Colony Grows

Years have passed and you no longer work for the Virginia Company. You buy some land in one of the new settlements along the river, beyond Jamestown. Many new settlers buy land there to farm. However, the company doesn't really own the land it is selling. It has taken it from the Algonquians. If a tribe is hostile, its village is destroyed, so it's safer for tribes to seem friendly. Secretly they are planning to wipe out the colonists. In March of 1622, the Algonquians massacre colonists all along the river. A warning from a friendly Algonquian saves Jamestown from total destruction.

Why are the Algonquians angry?

SETTLEMENTS are well protected with forts and storehouses. Fields are fenced off and each house has an enclosed yard for livestock.

ANGER GROWS as the Algonquians see more of their land being fenced off. They are told they cannot enter it without permission.

IN 1622, friendly looking Algonquian traders are invited in for breakfast. Suddenly they take their hosts' tools and attack.

Success!

Congratulations! You've worked hard to build yourself a home. Now you have a thriving farm. Life is getting easier. The Algonquians seem to be beaten and the colony has found that exporting tobacco to Europe is very profitable. Local Virginian tobacco is not very good, but a colonist

TOBACCO SMOKING reaches Europe from America in the 16th century. King James I thinks it's a filthy, harmful habit.

named John Rolfe experiments with growing other types. He is so successful that now, in the 1620s, tobacco is the colony's main crop. You hope to make your fortune by selling it. The future looks good, but remember that you have been lucky. In the colony's first 18 years, 7,289 colonists sailed for Virginia and 6,040 of those people died. Had you known the hardships you would face, would you still have wanted to be an American colonist?

IN THE 1620s Jamestown is a thriving little market town. People no longer fear living outside the fort. Now it is the Algonquians who are afraid.

INDEPENDENCE. Virginia makes its own laws. King James I is against this, but in 1619, the colonists hold the first elected "parliament" in the New World.

Glossary

Algonquians A Native American tribe that lived along the eastern side of North America.

Ambush A surprise attack from a hidden position.

Armada The powerful Spanish fleet that invaded England in 1588, but was defeated by the English and the Dutch.

Cannon A large gun that is attached to a platform for firing because of its size.

Clapboard Thin wooden boards for building. It is made by splitting timber vertically.

Colony A group of people who settle in a country far from their homeland.

Condemned When someone is found guilty of a crime and is given a punishment for it.

Courtier A servant of a royal court.

Dubbing When a king or queen makes a subject a knight, giving him the title "Sir."

Drought A lack of water causing crops to fail.

Fort A settlement that has protective walls and guarded gates, which can be defended easily.

Gentleman A man born into a family, which, unlike ordinary families, had the right to carry guns.

Gourd The large, hard-skinned fruit of a trailing plant, similar to a pumpkin.

Massacre When a large number of people are killed.

Native Someone who is living in the place they were born.

Omen A sign of future happiness or disaster.

Panning Searching for gold by rinsing soil in a pan to separate any particles of gold it may contain.

Provisions Supplies of food and other materials.

Publicity Getting people interested in someone or something.

Rebellion Fighting against the people in charge of something.

Stingray A flat fish with a tail that injects a poison, which affects the heart and nervous system.

Trinket A small or worthless ornament or piece of jewelry.

Yellow fever A disease that causes liver damage and turns the skin yellow.

Index

What Happened to Pocahontas?

In December 1607, Captain John Smith was captured by a Powhatan hunting party and eventually taken before the paramount chief. During this encounter, Pocahontas is said to have saved Smith's life (see more about this story on pages 18–19).

In April 1613, on a trading expedition to the Potomac River, Captain Samuel Argall kidnapped Pocahontas and brought her to Jamestown. Here she was baptized and given the Christian name Rebecca. In April 1614, she married John Rolfe, probably at Jamestown. Peaceful relations were established temporarily between the Powhatan people and the English. In 1616 John Rolfe, Pocahontas, and their infant son, Thomas, sailed to England to promote investment in Virginia. Pocahontas, known as "Lady Rebecca Rolfe," was entertained at the court of King James I and Queen Anne.

However, the damp English climate was not good for her health, and by March 1617 the Rolfe family was ready to return to Virginia.

This portrait is based on the only image of Pocahontas drawn from life.

Unfortunately, Pocahontas did not live long enough to even begin the voyage home. After traveling down the River Thames, Pocahontas, seriously ill, had to be taken ashore. Not far from London, England, Pocahontas died of an unspecified illness. Many historians believe she suffered from a respiratory ailment, such as pneumonia, while others think she may have died from dysentery. Pocahontas, only about 21 years old, was buried on March 21, 1617.

Her husband returned to America, remarried, and died in 1622. The son of John Rolfe and Pocahontas was raised in London, but he moved to Virginia around 1640 and got married there. His descendants married into leading Virginia families.

Laws of Jamestown

In 1611 Governor Thomas Dale brought in new laws for the Jamestown colony. Here are some of them, rephrased in modern English.

1. Twice a day, on working days, every man and woman must attend a religious service. The first time a person misses the service, his day's food will be kept from him. The second time, he will be whipped. The third time, he will be sent to the galleys for six months.

2. If anyone runs away from the colony to live with the Powhatan people or any other Indian chiefs, he or she will be executed.

3. No person shall criticize, disobey, or ignore the commands of the Governor or any other public official. The first time a person does so, he will be whipped three times; the second time, he will be sent to the galleys for a month; the third time, he will be executed.

4. Anyone who lies or bears false witness in any case, no matter who he is, shall be put to death.

5. No person shall steal, lose, or willingly break, or fraudulently make away, either spade, shovel, hatchet, axe, or other tool or instrument, upon pain of whipping.

6. No person shall throw out water or suds in the open street . . . upon pain of whipping.

Did You Know?

- Galleys were long ships with one deck and twenty to thirty oars on each side. The ship was driven across the water by the oars, with six or seven men per oar. Rowing in a galley was a common punishment for criminals.
- One man who stole a few pints of oatmeal had a needle jabbed through his tongue and was then chained to a tree until he starved.

Top 17th-Century Medicines

Seventeenth-century medicine called for the use of herbs in many remedies. Below are some of the most commonly used herbs, along with what 17th-century people believed about their capabilities.

Lemon balm This was put in wine. It was thought to be good against the bites of venomous animals, for comforting the heart, and for driving away melancholy and sadness.

Basil The juice was mixed with oil of roses, vinegar, and finely ground parched barley. It was considered good against "inflammations" and used to "clean away dimness of the eyes."

Sage This was thought to be good for the head and brain. It was used to sharpen the senses and memory and strengthen the sinuses.

Chives This was considered harmful to the eyes and brain, but good for thinning the blood.

A Recipe for Pottage

A common dish eaten by the Jamestown settlers was a thick soup called pottage. Here is a modern recipe to make it.

2 tablespoons bread crumbs
1 egg yolk
1 teaspoon chopped parsley
1 teaspoon salt

1 cup milk
a pinch of saffron
½ teaspoon ground ginger
1½ cup cooked peas

Beat together the bread crumbs, egg yolk, parsley, salt, ginger, and saffron. Next, bring the milk almost to a boil, and pour in the peas and bread crumb mixture. Bring to a boil over a low heat, stirring continuously.